men's
watches

in the same series

trainers, sandrine pereira
underdressed, élodie piveteau – philippe vaurès santamaria
mum's cooking for lads away from home, dominique ayral – jean-pierre cagnat

Translation by Translate-A-Book, Oxford

Design and creation: GRAPH' M/Nord Compo, France

ISBN: 2-7528-0242-0
Publisher code: T00242
Copyright registration: October 2005
Printed in Italy by Rotolito Lombarda

www.fitwaypublishing.com

Fitway Publishing
12, avenue d' Italie – 75627 Paris cedex 13, France

men's
watches

hervé borne

contents

preface

There is a certain *je ne sais quoi* about a beautiful watch on a man's wrist. Something special. Something *definitive*.

A beautiful watch is more – so *much* more – than a simple accessory. It is a statement and a mark of distinction.

Elegance may come naturally, but it can also be acquired. It is all a question of attitude. Of natural poise. Of spontaneous flair. Elegance implies individual style rather than a slavish adherence to passing trends. It is a function of choice and attention to detail, projecting and sustaining a personal image that sets an individual off from those around him. Elegance eschews the flamboyant in favour of the discreet, the ostentatious in favour of the understated. Elegance, in short, is a state of mind.

Elegance is also about *savoir-faire* and *savoir-vivre*: whatever the social context, today's man aspires to be perceived as handsome, well groomed and seductive, with carefully manicured nails, highly polished shoes, an immaculate haircut and beautifully cut clothes. Plus one indispensable accessory: a watch – the only jewellery a real man can and should wear.

An innate sense of elegance precludes wearing a chronograph with a tuxedo or strapping on an ultra-thin hand-wound mechanical timepiece to go jogging, let alone sporting an ostentatiously over-the-top watch during business hours. Lapses in taste are invariably noted and almost never forgotten or readily forgiven …

Accordingly, the seven chapters in this book are structured to evoke the seven days of the week and a succession of typical male activities. In each instance, a different type of watch is explored; arguably the 'right' watch for the 'right' occasion. In the final analysis, of course, it all boils down to personal taste and freedom of choice. The observations that follow are not intended as hard-and-fast rules but merely as recommendations: it must be for the individual to decide which model of watch is best suited to his own particular lifestyle and environment.

office hours ...

A typical start to a typical working week: trainers, casual trousers and weekend sweatshirts make way for city shoes, suits and perhaps even a collar and tie. In short, the uniform most of us wear at work.

A watch is an important accessory at work. Not any old watch, of course, but a watch that projects an active urban lifestyle.

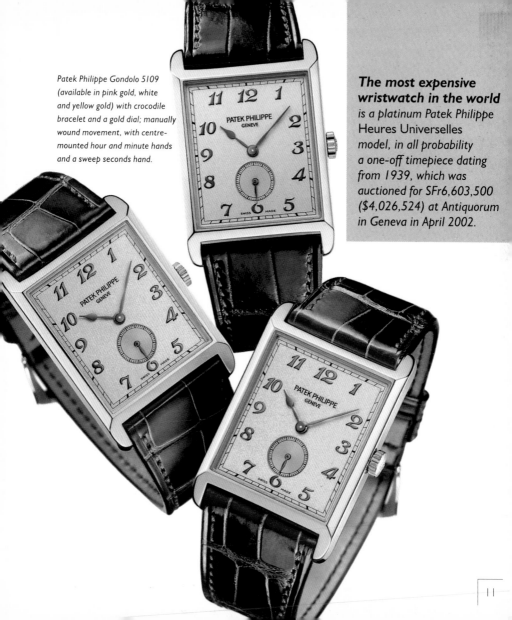

Patek Philippe Gondolo 5109 (available in pink gold, white and yellow gold) with crocodile bracelet and a gold dial; manually wound movement, with centre-mounted hour and minute hands and a sweep seconds hand.

The most expensive wristwatch in the world is a platinum Patek Philippe Heures Universelles model, in all probability a one-off timepiece dating from 1939, which was auctioned for SFr6,603,500 ($4,026,524) at Antiquorum in Geneva in April 2002.

A quartz watch *is a watch equipped with a battery-powered electronic movement.*

A self-winding watch *is a watch that automatically winds itself as a result of the movement of the wearer's wrist.*

A manually wound watch *is one whose mechanical spring is activated by rotating the crown of the winding mechanism situated on the casing.*

Opposite: *Longines Master Collection watch in steel with crocodile bracelet and chequer-patterned (guilloché) dial; automatic movement with centre-mounted hour, minute and seconds hands and a date display window.*

Page left: *Zenith Elite Class in steel with crocodile bracelet and silvered dial; extra-slim automatic movement featuring centre-mounted hour and minute hands, with a small seconds hand at centre left and a date display window.*

In other words, a 'dress watch' that has earned its place as a classic amid the incredible range of men's watches currently on the market. In terms of form and function, it is not particularly original and, above all, it is not ostentatious. It is much more a statement of discretion and sobriety. As far as form is concerned, the options are straightforward: round, square, rectangular or even a rounded rectangle, or perhaps something along the lines of the *tonneau* design, a cross between a rectangle and an oval shape that was all the rage in the Art Deco years of the 1930s. To this day, however, the round dial is still the most common shape, despite changing fashions that have impacted on watch design. It's not difficult to understand why. The round dial is perfectly adequate to house two hands rotating around a fixed central point for the 86,000 seconds, 1,400 minutes and 24 hours that make up each and every day of our lives.

Dubey & Schaldenbrand Aerodyn Trophée in pink gold with crocodile bracelet and chequered dial; automatic movement with centre-mounted hour, minute and seconds hands.

That said, sporting a *tonneau*-style watch confers on the wearer a certain air of 'dandyism', which is quite acceptable in the urban context. And square and rectangular dials convey yet another form of personal style and elegance. These considerations are far from negligible, bearing in mind the well-known fact that among the first things a woman will notice about a man are his hands, his shoes – and, of course, his watch … Round, square, rectangular, *tonneau* – all basic shapes, but all somehow *reasonable*. The casing shouldn't be too thick and the dimensions should be kept within discreet limits. Anything more ostentatious should be reserved for leisure-time activities. Watch case materials are essentially simple, with stainless steel far and away the material of choice, not least

Page right: *Guy Ellia Time Square in white gold, with gold dial and crocodile bracelet; automatic movement featuring centre-mounted hour and minute hands and a set back seconds hand.*

Double page overleaf: *From the Rolex Prince range: white or pink gold with crocodile bracelets and guilloché dials; manually wound movement with centre-mounted hour and minute hands and a small seconds hand at bottom centre.*

office hours ...

because of its attractive silver colour, its clean finish and robust qualities, not to mention the cost advantages compared with gold or platinum. Not that gold is unacceptable in a dress watch – far from it: grey or white gold for that understated look, yellow gold for the classically minded, or even a tinge of pink to project a *Dolce Vita* image. (As it happens, pink gold has been around for quite some time now and is very fashionable in Italy …) Platinum is best held in reserve for evenings on the town. The metal is as expensive as a precious stone and tends to weigh heavily on the wrist when worn all day. Then there are the newcomers to the watch industry, among them titanium and high-tech ceramics. These are extremely robust and scratchproof, with a distinctive appearance that is more suitable for the sporty look.

Page right: *Chopard LUC Twin, available in white or yellow gold with black or white brass dial and crocodile bracelet; automatic movement with centre-mounted hour, minute and seconds hands and a date display window.*

Double page overleaf, left: *Hublot Elegant model in steel with a black dial and a natural rubber bracelet; automatic movement featuring centre-mounted hour, minute and seconds hands and a porthole date display window.* Right: *Hublot Classic in yellow gold with a black dial and a natural rubber bracelet; automatic movement with centre-mounted hour, minute and seconds hands and a porthole date display window.*

office hours ...

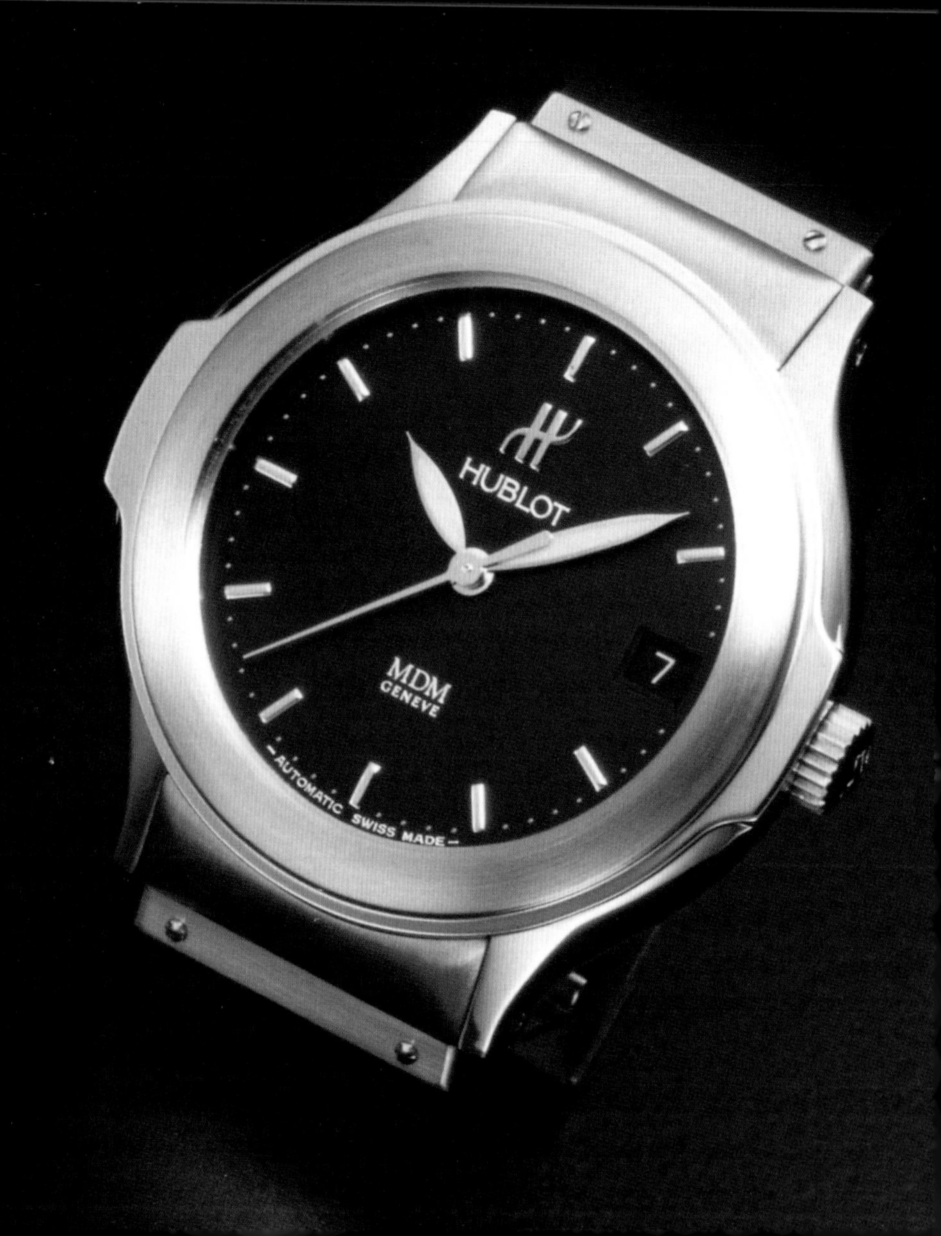

Left: François-Paul Journe precision platinum chronometer with a crocodile bracelet and guilloché dial; manually wound movement with centre-mounted hour and minute hands, a power reserve indicator at centre right and a small seconds hand at bottom left (7 o'clock).

F.P.JOURNE
Invenit et Fecit

The most expensive pocket watch collector's item in the world is a Patek Philippe named after Henry Graves, the billionaire banker who commissioned it in 1928. The piece was delivered in 1933. The casing in yellow gold houses a 24-part mechanical movement. The watch was auctioned at Sotheby's in New York in December 1999, when it fetched a price of $11,002,500.

Right: Eterna 1935 in steel with a crocodile bracelet and a silvered dial; automatic movement with centre-mounted hour, minute and seconds hands and a date display window.

When it comes to dress watches, there is by no means a plethora of options for straps and bracelets. Leather remains the order of the day, with metal, rubber and Kevlar® straps resolutely leisure-time options. Fabric straps appear feminine and effeminate (except for satin, which goes well with evening dress). When one speaks of 'leather', however, it need not necessarily be of the box-calf variety. In fact, the permutations are virtually infinite: smooth or embossed, matt or polished alligator, or less common exotic varieties such as *galuchat*.

Jaeger-leCoultre Master Control in pink gold with a crocodile bracelet and silvered dial; automatic movement with centre-mounted hour, minute and seconds hands and a date display window.

The 'limited edition' concept *was the brainchild of Swatch Group supremo Nicolas G. Hayek. When the Swatch range was first launched in 1983, he hit on the idea of issuing individual series that were limited or numbered.*

As far as colour is concerned, flamboyant shades are only for fashion victims, and the male colour palette rarely extends beyond black and brown. Brown leather ages beautifully in contact with the skin and black goes with almost everything. The more adventurous may opt for grey or even dark blue: two chromatic alternatives that are perfect adjuncts to a flannel suit worn with a white shirt. Even claret or gold is acceptable in the summer months.

A watch is a fashion accessory in its own right, and it has often been said that it is the only item of jewellery a man should ever wear. That particular cliché is somewhat out of date now, with the advent of all manner of male jewellery, and it should not be allowed to detract from the primary function of a watch, namely to record time and show it accurately.

Page right: *IWC Portofino in pink gold with crocodile bracelet and black or white dial; automatic movement with centre-mounted hour, minute and seconds hands and a date display window.*

Double page overleaf, left: *Cartier Pasha 42 in white gold with a silvered opaline dial and a crocodile bracelet; automatic movement with centre-mounted hour, minute and seconds hands.* Right: *Vacheron Constantin Royal: a chronometer in grey gold with silvered dial and crocodile bracelet; automatic movement with centre-mounted hour, minute and seconds hands and a date display window.*

In fact, watches ideally record hours, minutes, seconds and, more often than not, the date. Accordingly, the watch dials – irrespective of whether the watch itself is hand-wound or self-winding, mechanical, automatic or quartz – are distinguished by their functionality and their provision of essential data. Two centrally positioned hands show the hours and minutes and, usually, a further tiny hand (typically offset near the six o'clock point) will count off the seconds. As for the date, this is usually shown in Arabic numerals in a window aperture set close to the three o' clock point.

Parmigiani Fleurier Forma XL in steel with a crocodile bracelet and guilloché dial; manually wound movement with centre-mounted hour, minute and seconds hands and a trailing date display.

office hours ...

Page left: *Zenith Elite Class in steel with a crocodile bracelet and a guilloché silvered dial; ultra-thin automatic movement with centre-mounted hour and minute hands, a small seconds hand at centre left and a date display window.*

Below left: *Hermès Arceau model in steel with leather strap and brown dial; automatic movement with centre-mounted hour and minute hands and a date display window.* Right: *Auguste Reymond Boogie model in steel with leather strap and white dial; manually wound movement with centre-mounted hour and minute hands, a small seconds hand at bottom centre and a date display window.*

Patek Philippe,
the brand of excellence

Philippe Stern, president of Patek Philippe, doesn't mince words: 'If you are in the market for a Patek Philippe, you are among those who admire excellence. For you a time-piece is much more than an instrument that merely shows the time. To acquire a Patek Philippe is to acquire a share in our artistic and technological heritage.' The full import of

Opposite (from
left to right):
*Philippe and Thierry
Stern, president
and vice-president
respectively
of Patek Philippe.*

Page right:
*Calatrava Clou
de Paris in yellow
gold with a white
dial; manually
wound movement
with centre-
mounted hour
and minute hands.*

these words can best be exemplified by taking a closer look at the history of Patek Philippe, Geneva's sole-surviving independent watchmaker. In 1839, Antoine-Norbert de Patek set up the workshop of Patek, Czapek & Cie. From that day onwards, each Patek Philippe timepiece has been, quite simply, a work of art. Antoine-Norbert de Patek's speciality was top-of-the-range pocket watches until he visited Paris in 1844 and met Jean-Adrien Philippe,

Left: *Calatrava model in yellow gold with a crocodile bracelet and a silvered dial; automatic movement with centre-mounted hour and minute hands.*

Centre: *Officer's timepiece in yellow gold with a crocodile bracelet and a white dial; automatic movement with centre-mounted hour, minute and seconds hands and a date display window. The back of the case opens like a pocket watch.*

Right: *Antoine-Norbert de Patek (above) and Adrien Philippe (below).*

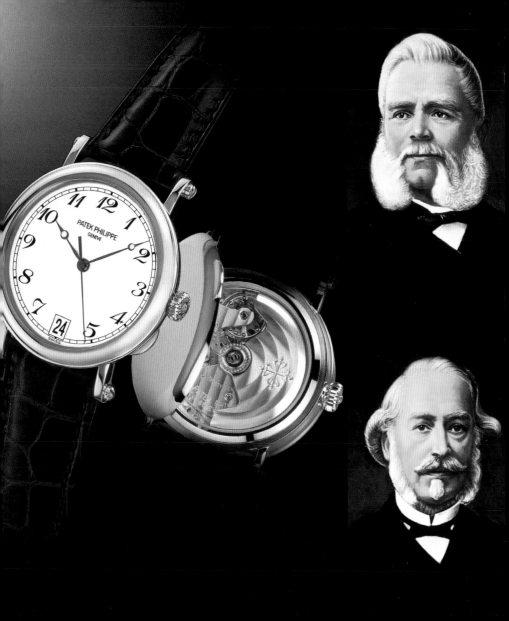

the son of a clockmaker and a technical innovator. The two men joined forces the following year and Philippe rapidly transformed the original Patek workshop by mechanising its production processes. That was only the beginning. In 1845, the pair patented their design for an integrated winder and adjuster. In London in 1851, they exhibited the world's smallest watch. In 1868, they created the first Swiss wristwatch. And, in the 1870s, mechanical movements perfected by Patek Philippe won awards at competitions organised by the Geneva Observatory. Today, their tradition of craftsmanship is complemented by a system of rigorous quality control to guarantee the standards that gave Patek Philippe its name. The brand masterminds and integrates each production phase from conception to final assembly, including movement, casing and strap/bracelet design. Producing a Patek Philippe involves 32 specialist disciplines and, on average, requires 1,500 separate operations. This commitment to perfection is shared by the firm's nine hundred employees housed in the new Patek Philippe facility set up in Geneva in 1996. The firm's quest for excellence continues undiluted. Patek Philippe is now acknowledged as the creator *par excellence* of the dress watch, with the classical lines and unparalleled elegance of its iconic Calatrava range.

Opposite: *Calatrava Clou de Paris in yellow gold with an enamel dial; manually wound movement with centre-mounted hour and minute hands and a small seconds hand at bottom centre.*

Below: *Detail of two of the manufactory workshops, one (above) given over to decoration, the other (below) to engraving the distinctive Calatrava Cross logo on the watch movement.*

The workday is nearly over and the office gradually empties.
Those unread files can wait until tomorrow. It is time now for
a spot of relaxation. But punctuality is of the essence, never more
so than when you're scheduled to meet an inveterate watch collector whose overriding passion is Time Itself and the instruments
that record it …

The Cartier Tortue XL:
a single press-stud tourbillon
model in platinum with a crocodile
bracelet and two inset enamel
counters; manually wound movement
with centre-mounted hour and minute
hands and a small seconds hand.

This is a true aficionado, a dedicated collector who is totally conversant with the ins and outs of watches and timepieces. Accordingly, it's important to choose your own watch with care. Not any old watch will do. Quite the contrary. A classic dress watch that merely shows the hours, minutes, seconds and (perhaps) the date is *not* an option. To rise to the occasion, the watch on your wrist should be a complex affair, a timepiece that has a certain lyricism combined with a respect for tradition and an appreciation of excellence. To put it another way, a timepiece with 'complications' – special features that will excite even the most knowledgeable connoisseur.

__2004 turnover of the watch and clockmaking industry in Germany__ was some €559 million; of this figure, however, a mere 24% related to watch manufacture, with 15% going to clocks and clock movements and 61% attributable to components, including straps and bracelets.

An Audemars Piguet Jules Audemars tourbillon chronometer in grey gold with a crocodile bracelet and two inset silvered counters; manually wound movement with centre-mounted hour and minute hands and a small seconds hand.

But what exactly does a collector mean by 'complications'?

The answer is unequivocal: a mechanical hand-wound or self-winding timepiece that offers at least one additional function over and above the standard functions noted earlier. And, as any high-end watch collector worth his salt will agree, those features really make all the difference. In essence, there are seven prime categories of supplementary functions which fit the bill: chronograph functions; a power reserve indicator; a perpetual calendar; a minute repeater; an 'hour-jump' function (see below); a vortex; a fly-back hand.

As a result, today's watch faces frequently display a bewildering array of functions and features that are deemed useful to varying degrees to the modern male.

Blancpain's Le Brassus:
a perpetual timepiece in pink gold
with a crocodile bracelet and an
opaline dial; automatic movement
with centre-mounted hour and
minute hands, a time zone indicator
and date display, day-and-month
windows, a small seconds hand
and a lunar phase indicator.

Their lyricism and splendour are a collector's delight and aficio-nados will go to inconceivable lengths to get their hands on them – typically by bidding at specialist watch auctions such as the one organised in April 2005 by Antiquorum in Geneva to mark the 250th anniversary of the Vacheron Constantin manufactory. That event generated sales totalling more than SFr18 million.

By far the world's largest watchmaker group *is the Swatch Group under the overall management of Nicolas G Hayek. Eighteen brands belong to the group, ranging from Breguet to Swatch by way of Omega, Blancpain, Longines and other household names. In 2004, the Swatch Group sold a total of 125 million units; group turnover for the year was more than SFr4 billion.*

Blancpain's single press-stud chronograph in white gold with a crocodile bracelet and a brown dial with three inset counters; automatic movement with centre-mounted hours and minutes, a seconds hand and a date display window.

Among the 250 items auctioned, a minute-repeater from 1827 fetched SFr132,000, a 1962 chronograph went for SFr100,000 and a 1990 *tourbillon* was acquired for SFr413,680. A further high-light of the April 2005 event was the sale of the minute-repeater cum perpetual calendar model acquired by King Fouad in 1914, which tipped the scales at SFr3 million!

All this is a far cry from the days when high-end watches appeared to be in danger of being relegated to the status of museum pieces as a result of the quartz invasion spearheaded by Asian countries. Today, mass commercial production exists side-by-side with top-of-the-range watch manufacture. What is more, the time-worn ritual of taking the crown or winding stem between thumb and forefinger and conscientiously winding one's watch each morning (taking due care not to overwind and damage the mainspring) has made quite a comeback: it would seem that the 'vintage' watch has lost precious little of its appeal …

Blancpain's single press-stud chronograph with transparent sapphire base displaying the M.185 automatic movement.

Zenith Elite Class in steel with a crocodile bracelet and a silvered guilloché dial; ultra-slim automatic movement with centre-mounted hour and minute hands, a power reserve indicator, a small seconds hand at centre left and a date display window.

Page right: Zenith Grande Class chronograph in white gold with a crocodile bracelet and a grey dial with two inset counters; automatic movement with centre-mounted hour and minute hands and reset function, and a date display window.

Zenith Grande Class
chronograph in white
gold with a rubber
bracelet, a black dial
and two inset counters;
automatic movement
with centre-mounted
hour, minute and
seconds hands and
a date display window.

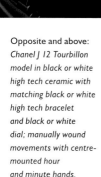

Opposite and above:
Chanel J 12 Tourbillon
model in black or white
high tech ceramic with
matching black or white
high tech bracelet
and black or white
dial; manually wound
movements with centre-
mounted hour
and minute hands.

Double page overleaf: Recto and
verso of Richard Mille's Tourbillon
RM 009 model in Alusic (a silicon,
carbon and aluminium alloy) with
rubber bracelet and transparent
sapphire dial. The manually wound
movement with centre-mounted
hour and minute hands is visible
through the sapphire base.

a glass or two with an aficionado …

a glass or two with an aficionado …

Before meeting up with one's collector friend, however, it is as well to reflect on some of the classic 'complications' – the supplementary time mechanisms – that exert so much appeal.

The **chronograph** is the most widespread function and can be used for all kinds of elapsed time measurement. Chronographs are so common now that they are even available in quartz configurations. The chronograph has a mechanism incorporating analogue or digitally displayed sub-dials with an independent second hand that rotates one revolution per minute and can be started, stopped or returned to zero by depressing buttons on the case. Fractions of a second, seconds, minutes, hours and even days of elapsed time can be recorded and displayed in this way.

The **power reserve indicator** is a very practical feature on a mechanical watch. Like the petrol gauge in a car, it shows how much longer the watch will operate before it has to be wound again.

The **perpetual calendar** displays the day of the week, the date, the month, the year and, frequently, the phases of the moon. It automatically corrects to take account of leap years.

Preceding double page: *Vacheron Constantin's Jubilee 1755 shown in four variants in pink, yellow or grey gold and platinum, with crocodile bracelets and a guilloché dial; automatic movement with centre-mounted hour, minute and seconds hands, a power reserve indicator and a day and date display. Produced in a limited series of 500 for each gold variant and 250 in platinum.*

Opposite: *Aficionado wearing an elegant Zenith Grande Class chronograph in white gold, featuring a reset dial and a date display window.*

a glass or two with an aficionado …

The **minute-repeater** is a function that uses tiny hammers to strike and chime the time of day. When the time is 4:47, the watch will chime four times for the hours, three times to indicate three quarters and, finally, twice for the additional two minutes.

The **hour-jump** is a splendid feature. Here, the face boasts only a single needle – the minute hand – and a window aperture (normally located in the top of the dial) in which Arabic numerals are used to 'jump' the hour from one to the next.

In 1506, Pietro Guido de Mantoue, the most skilful small-scale horologist of his era, created the first pocket watch.

Preceding double page, left: *Patek Philippe Travel Time* in gold with a crocodile bracelet and a silvered dial; manually wound movement with centre-mounted hour, minute and seconds hands and a secondary time zone indicator, with a small seconds hand and a 24-hour display. Right: A *Harry Winston Opus V* in pink gold with crocodile bracelet and three-dimensional dial; manually wound movement with satellite hour and minute counters, day–night display and a power reserve indicator.

Page right: *Piaget's Emperador:* a pink gold tourbillon timepiece with a crocodile bracelet and a silvered guilloché dial. The manually wound movement features centre-mounted hour and minute hands and a power reserve indicator.

Baselworld, the most important watch fair of the year, is held in the Swiss city of Basel and, together with the SIHH (Salon International de la Haute Horlogerie), is the focus and Mecca of the international watch industry. Hall One of Baselworld brings together the most prestigious exhibitors such as Patek Philippe, Rolex and Blancpain, while the SIHH exhibits the full Richemont Group range, together with that of a number of independents such as Audemars Piguet or Roger Dubuis.

The **tourbillon** was the brainchild of Abraham-Louis Breguet and was invented to eliminate positional timekeeping errors. It may be described as a regulating device that cancels the effects of gravity on the precision of a mechanical watch movement by ensuring each minute a complete rotation of the balance, lever and escapement around a single axis. The tourbillon is generally regarded as extremely difficult to manufacture. It was originally conceived for pocket watches and is only very infrequently incorporated into today's wristwatches. That said, it is a collector's delight and at the same time is further evidence of the watchmaker's *savoir faire*.

The **fly-back hand** is a second superimposed hand on a chronograph and is used, for example, to calculate intermediary (lap) times or determine finishing times for more than one competitor in a race. When stopped and reset to zero, the hand literally 'flies back'.

Vacheron Constantin's minute-repeater Tour de l'Île tourbillon model: a pink gold timepiece with a twin (recto/verso) dial in silvered and ornamented gold and a crocodile bracelet. The manually wound movement features on the reverse hour, minute and seconds displays, a power reserve indicator, a secondary time zone display and a lunar phase display. The model was fabricated in a limited series of seven.

The world's most 'complex' watch is the Patek Philippe Calibre 89, a white gold 'skeleton' pocket watch which boasts no fewer than 33 individual movement components, visible through both faces of the casing. The Calibre 89 is one of the five most expensive watches in the world; one auctioned by Antiquorum in April 2004 fetched SFr6,603,500 ($5,002,652).

Page left: *Octo Incontro* tourbillon model by *Gérald Genta* featuring a crocodile bracelet and a cloisonné ceramic dial; automatic movement with centre-mounted flyback hour and minute hands. On the reverse, digitally displayed ancillary functions via a second, multifunction quartz-powered movement.

Opposite: *Daniel Roth's perpetual calendar* model in platinum, with a crocodile bracelet and a black and white dial; automatic movement with eccentric hour and minute display, a lunar phase feature, day-and-month display windows, a date pointer and a leap-year display.

Vacheron Constantin, elder statesman

Vacheron Constantin ranks as the oldest watch manufactory in the world. In 2005, this venerable firm celebrated the 250th anniversary of its unbroken activity.

1755 was the year of Marie Antoinette's birth. Back then, Vacheron, the brilliant young horologist, borrowed the princely sum of 1,000 *livres* to underwrite a workshop in the heart of Geneva. This *cabinotier* – as Geneva's clockmakers were known in those days – promptly started to turn out exceptional timepieces, including what is generally regarded as his first-ever creation – a silver pocket watch engraved with the inscription *J: MC Vacheron Constantin à Genève*. The quality of Vacheron's work was widely admired not only in Geneva but elsewhere in Europe. In 1819, a shrewd businessman and peerless dealer called François Constantin joined forces with Vacheron's heirs and travelled the length and breadth of Europe in search of new markets.

Left: *The marque's earliest-known silver pocket watch (dating from 1755) is on show at the Vacheron Constantin Museum in Geneva.*

Right: *François Constantin and Jean-Marc Vacheron.*

FRANÇOIS CONSTANTIN
1788   1854

JEAN-MARC VACHERON
1731 * 1805

The Vacheron Constantin Manufactory was now well and truly launched. In 1839 Georges-Auguste Leschot was hired as the firm's technical director. Leschot was an extremely gifted engineer and a visionary who developed new machinery and equipment to permit serial fabrication of movement components. Watch manufacture was revolutionised. Throughout the 20th century, creations by Vacheron Constantin went from strength to strength in artistic innovation and commercial success. A Vacheron Constantin timepiece has always been a permutation of three key factors. First, *technique*, based on two and a half centuries of craftsmanship combined with state-of-the-art production equipment (timepieces are based on a movement range that runs the gamut from the simplest to the most complex, including models with perpetual calendars, moonphase displays, hour-jumps, tourbillons and minute-repeaters). Second, a refined, understated and timeless *aesthetic* sense. And third but by no means least, exceptional added value in terms of *quality of finish*. Today, 80% of Vacheron Constantin output is of the mechanical variety. The firm has in excess of 350 employees worldwide, 250 of whom work in Switzerland. The firm has two

Top left: *Gold manually-wound pocket chronometer dating from 1915.* Right: *Double-display chronograph in pink gold (limited edition of eight; 1956).*

Bottom left: *Detail of a manually wound movement.* Centre: *Unique clock created for the 250th anniversary of Vacheron Constantin. Christened 'Esprit des Cabinotiers', it was sold at auction on 3rd April 2005 for €1,430,000.* Right: *The elegant finish and mechanical complexity of the Vacheron Constantin movement are visible through the transparent sapphire case.*

complementary production facilities, one at Plan-les-Ouates near Geneva, which came on stream in August 2004, and the other in the Vallée de Joux. Together, these two sites generate some fifteen thousand pieces annually, a figure that attests to the firm's dedication to quality as opposed to quantity. Vacheron Constantin is in a league of its own as the elder statesman of complication models and as a representative of high-end watchmaking at its sophisticated best.

Below: A movement assembly workshop at the Plan-les-Ouates site.

Page right: Platinum Saint-Gervais tourbillon model with a crocodile bracelet and a guilloché dial. The manually wound movement features centre-mounted hour and minute hands, a six-hour seconds display, a date display, a double power reserve indicator and a full perpetual calendar. The series is limited to 55 units.

WEDNESDAY, 1 P.M.

business lunch …

It is midweek and things are ticking over nicely at the office. Last weekend seems ages ago and next weekend is still some time away. For some people, the pace is too hectic and they seem to have too much on their plate. Others, however, are content to take things in their stride and take each day as it comes.

It is close to one o'clock and a quick glance at the desk diary confirms a business lunch scheduled for any minute now.

A deal is in the offing and it is important to be in a positive frame of mind and project a strong image …

Selecting the right watch for the occasion is part of role-playing. Nothing too flamboyant, but one that asserts itself, makes a statement, acts as a status symbol. In a nutshell, a watch that has a decades-long track record, a watch that adorns the wrists of movers and shakers the world over, a watch that has the inherent capacity to project self-awareness and leadership …

An *icon*. There are those who might argue that 'a watch is a watch and that's all there is to it', but others know that's not so.

Preceding page: Breguet's Type XXI: *a timepiece in pink gold with a crocodile bracelet and a brown dial with three counters; the automatic movement has centre-mounted hour and minute hands, a date display window and a special 'flyback' feature.*

Page right: *Tag Heuer ambassador Brad Pitt, pictured here wearing the celebrated Monaco Chronograph.*

There are watches that have impact, watches that are redolent of history. Back in the earliest days of aviation, the Brazilian-born pioneer Alberto Santos-Dumont decided he needed a wristwatch he could conveniently refer to in flight. His friend Louis Cartier came up with his first wristwatch in 1904 and promptly christened it the Santos. It was recently reissued to commemorate its hundredth anniversary in 2004 and its impact was immediate and sensational: nothing, it seemed, could compare with wearing the 'same' watch as one of aviation's most celebrated figures.

In addition to market leader Swatch, two other luxury goods manufacturers are major players: the Richemont Group owns Cartier, Dunhill, Vacheron Constantin, Panerai, Van Cleef & Arpels, Baume & Mercier, Piaget, Montblanc, Jaeger-leCoultre, A Lang & Söhne and IWC, while the LVMH Group owns TAG Heuer, Zenith, Chaumet, Fred, and the Dior and Louis Vuitton brands.

Right: *Cartier's Santos 100 in gold and steel, an automatic released in 2004 to mark the centenary of Louis Cartier's first wristwatch, created in 1904 for Cartier's friend Alberto Santos-Dumont, left.*

Then, in the 1930s, when the Art Deco movement was at its height, British officers stationed in India were irritated by the fact that their wristwatches were too easily damaged when they indulged in polo, their favourite pastime. This time around, it was Jaeger-leCoultre who came up with the idea of producing a watch with a reversible casing, thereby enabling the dial to be protected. The Reverso was born and is still one of Jaeger-leCoultre's top-selling models, each true to its original identity. Leonardo Di Caprio simply adores his …

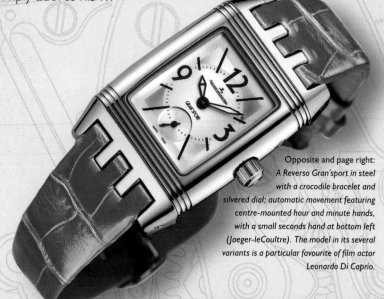

Opposite and page right:
A Reverso Gran'sport in steel with a crocodile bracelet and silvered dial; automatic movement featuring centre-mounted hour and minute hands, with a small seconds hand at bottom left (Jaeger-leCoultre). The model in its several variants is a particular favourite of film actor Leonardo Di Caprio.

Opposite:
*Reverso Grande GMT
in steel with a reversible
casing, crocodile bracelet
and double-face black dial;
manually wound movement
with (verso) hours, minutes
and small seconds display,
a large date display and
a day–night indicator.
The recto features
a secondary time zone
counter, a 24-hour display,
a power reserve indicator
and a Jaeger-leCoultre
time differential display
referenced to Greenwich Mean
Time (GMT).*

Page right: *Erstwhile
Jaeger-leCoultre brochure
extolling the originality
of the Reverso model.*

The **Qualité Fleurier Certification** issued by the Qualité Fleurier Foundation, set up in June 2001, is a designation common to brands produced in Fleurier by Chopard, Parmigiani Fleurier, Bovet and the Vaucher Manufactory and represents a common commitment to the establishment of new aesthetic and technical criteria. Formal certification, available as of 27 September 2004, denotes the attainment of standards of precision, reliability, durability and finish as determined by four separate quality-control processes conducted in Fleurier.

reciation

On 21 July 1969, the world held its breath as Neil Armstrong took his first tentative steps on the surface of the Moon, the culmination of the Apollo XI space mission. Armstrong was wearing an Omega Speedmaster and, ever since, the model been touted as 'the watch that walked on the Moon'. To this day, the Omega is standard NASA issue and ranks as an Omega masterpiece.

Watches have captivated leading figures all over the world – film stars, politicians, crowned heads and the like – and the public at large has sat up and taken notice.

Omega promotional material heralding the Speedmaster model's adoption as the official NASA timepiece.

Cartier's legendary Tank model was a case in point. It attained iconic status and was worn by prominent personalities such as Yves Saint Laurent, Andy Warhol, Lambert Wilson, Alain Prost, Alain Delon, Warren Beatty and Yves Montand.

Meanwhile, over at Longines, the *leitmotif* was 'Elegance is Attitude'. Diplomats and leading politicians quickly got the message, as did such diverse figures as actor Billy Zane (the 'bad guy' in *Titanic*) and Formula 1 driver Pedro Diniz.

The only watch ever to have 'walked' on the Moon was the Omega Speedmaster worn by Neil Armstrong during his lunar landing in 1969.

Page left: Yves Saint Laurent.

Opposite: The Tank, Cartier's signature model, shown here in its classic version in yellow gold with a manually wound movement; the Tank and its variants have featured on the wrists of celebrities the world over ...

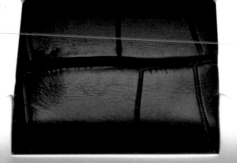

Opposite: *Cartier's manually wound Santos-Dumont in pink gold, another model launched in 2004 to mark the centenary of Louis Cartier's first wristwatch, created in 1904 for Cartier's friend Alberto Santos-Dumont.*

Page right: *'Elegance is an attitude': Actor Billy Zane, ambassador and front-man for the Longines marque.*

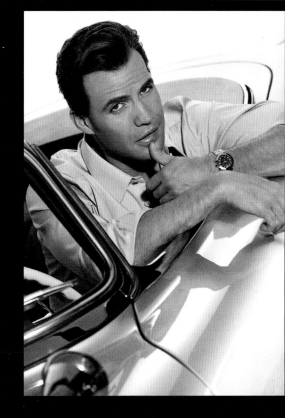

Steve McQueen sported a TAG Heuer in *Le Mans*, shot in 1971, and the firm immediately recognised the marketing potential with a general public increasingly in search of on-screen role models. It is no coincidence that TAG Heuer has turned to Brad Pitt to front its most recent advertising campaign. The same line of reasoning has inspired Breitling to use John Travolta and Wyler Vetta to sign up Richard Gere.

The Geneva stamp
or die was adopted by the Geneva Watchmakers' Guild on 6 November 1886. Its appearance on the backplate and on one of the bridges certifies that the movement has been assembled and regulated within the Swiss Canton of Geneva and connotes conformity with a 12-point code of technical excellence and quality elaborated according to the finest traditions of Swiss watchmaking craftsmanship.

A TAG Heuer Monaco Chronograph
in steel, with a crocodile bracelet and
three counters in optional black or white;
automatic movement with centre-
mounted hour and minute hands
and a date display window.

Opposite: *The TAG
Heuer Monaco in steel
with a rubber bracelet
and black dial; automatic
movement with centre-
mounted hour and minute
hands, a small seconds
hand and a date display
window.*

Page right: *Actor Steve
McQueen wore the
original TAG Heuer
Monaco in the film
Le Mans.*

Double page overleaf, page left:
*A Breitling Montbrillant chronograph
in steel with crocodile bracelet and black
dial with two inset counters; manually
wound movement with centre-mounted
hour and minute hands and a date
display window.* Page right: *Actor John
Travolta takes to the air in association
with Breitling, a marque that has
specialised in aviation timepieces ...*

business lunch ...

PROFESSION: PILOT
CAREER: ACTOR

Photographed by Patricia von Ah on the private runway
of the Travolta residence in Ocala, Florida.

" I LIKE TO FLY AT LEAST ONCE A DAY. "

People are acquainted with the star, the multi-faceted actor. But John
Travolta is also a seasoned pilot with more than 5,000 flight hours
under his belt, and is certified on eight different aircraft, including the
Boeing 747-400 Jumbo Jet. As a young boy in New Jersey, he already
used to dream of flying as he watched planes criss-crossing the sky
around the New York airports. Today, John Travolta travels the world at
the controls of his own airliner and nurtures a passion for everything
that embodies the authentic spirit of aviation. Like BREITLING wrist
instruments. Founded in 1884, BREITLING has shared all the finest hours
in aeronautical history. Models such as the NAVITIMER have become cult
objects for pilots the world over. Where safety is of crucial importance,
BREITLING is known as the specialist in reliable and high-performance
"wrist instruments" designed and tested for the most demanding
professionals. BREITLING chronographs meet the highest standards of
sturdiness and functionality, and are equipped with movements that are
chronometer-certified by the COSC (Swiss Official Chronometer
Testing Institute) – the highest reference in terms of precision and
reliability. One simply does not become an aviation supplier by chance.

BREITLING
1884

WWW.BREITLING.COM

INSTRUMENTS FOR PROFESSIONALS®

101

Opposite:
A Wyler Vetta
Espacité chronograph
in steel with crocodile
bracelet and a black dial with
three inset counters in red;
automatic movement with
centre-mounted hour and
minute hands and a date
display window.

Page right: Actor
Richard Gere sporting a
Wyler Vetta model on
behalf of his personal
charity, which benefited
to the tune of thirty
Euros for each model
sold in France, Italy or
Switzerland between
November 2004 and
November 2005.

L'importante è essere belli dentro.

Il fascino di un orologio Wyler Vetta non è semplice esteriorità. Da più di cento anni, dietro l'inconfondibile eleganza dello stile italiano, si nasconde l'eccellenza dell'orologeria svizzera. Perché fermarsi alle apparenze?

Per ogni orologio venduto, Wyler Vetta donerà una somma pari a 30 euro alla fondazione benefica di Richard Gere. Info su www.healingthedivide.com

Richard Gere indossa modello Espacité Crono Automatico Gran Data. www.wylervetta.ch

WYLER VETTA

— SWISS MADE. ITALIAN HERITAGE. SINCE 1896 —

Some 'trendy' timepieces have been around for decades, and have changed very little over the years. The Italian brand Panerai has been the official supplier to that country's navy ever since the beginning of the 20th century. During the Second World War, the Panerai was standard issue for Italian divers and commandos, and the original crown-protector design has been preserved down through the years in what is surely *the* military watch *par excellence*.

In 1926, Rolex came up with the world's first-ever water-resistant watch, the Oyster. The casing design has not changed since. This is arguably the most celebrated timepiece in the world and the name is widely recognised.

The Breguet Manufactory, named after founder Abraham-Louis Breguet – often cited as the 'founding father of fine watchmaking' – has produced numerous models that live up to the illustrious signature decorating the dial. Breguet's Type XX Chronograph models celebrated their 50th anniversary in 2005.

A Luminor by Panerai: steel with a leather strap and a brown dial; manually wound movement with centre-mounted hour and minute hands and a small seconds hand at centre left.

Audemars Piguet was the first house to market a deluxe sports watch. The Royal Oak is a stainless steel model that has carried a substantial price tag ever since its launch in 1972. It caused quite a stir in the marketplace even back then, and it continues to be the signature model in the Audemars Piguet range. It now exists in various versions, each instantly recognisable.

The Italian watchmaker and jeweller, Bvlgari, launched the Bvlgari-Bvlgari model in 1977 and had the temerity to proclaim the name twice around the bezel. This clear and unmistakable signature made its mark and the watch is the number-one bestseller in the Bvlgari range to this day, almost thirty years on!

A Bvlgari-Bvlgari in yellow gold with a crocodile bracelet and a black dial; automatic movement with centre-mounted hour, minute and seconds hands, a date display window.

An Audemars
Piguet Royal Oak, with
a steel strap and a blue guilloché
dial; automatic movement with
centre-mounted hour, minute
and seconds hands and a date
display window.

Rolex, universal icon

Rolex is a world-beater, instantly recognisable everywhere and the envy even of those who profess little interest in watches.

The brand was the brainchild of a young Bavarian named Hans Wilsdorf, who set up a watch distribution company in London in 1905. Fob watches were still all the range at the time, but Wilsdorf decided to stake his reputation on wristwatches. His innovative designs soon found favour with a younger clientele. In 1908, Wilsdorf came up with the brand name 'Rolex' and had it engraved on the dial. The name was simple, easily remembered and readily pronounceable in any language whatsoever. A myth was born.

From the onset, Rolex staked its reputation on quality and precision. Its efforts were rewarded in 1910, when it secured a Swiss Chronometry Control certificate, the first time such recognition had been bestowed on a wristwatch. In 1914, the Royal Observatory at Kew awarded Rolex a Class A certificate of precision. From that point onwards, Rolex and precision were virtually synonymous. In 1919, Hans Wilsdorf founded Montres Rolex SA, with his corporate headquarters in Geneva.

Left: *The new Daytona Chronograph in grey gold, with a grey gold bracelet and a red and anthracite dial with three inset counters; automatic movement with centre-mounted hour and minute hands.*

Top right: *Hans Wilsdorf.* Centre: *André J. Heiniger.* Bottom: *Patrick Heiniger.*

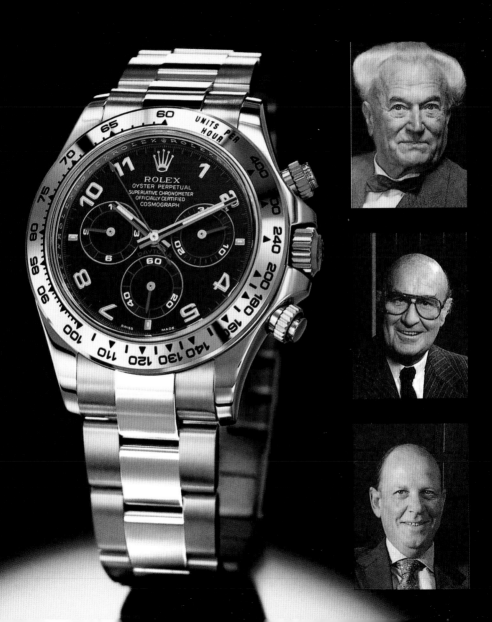

Act Two of the Rolex saga dates from 1926, when Rolex came up with the world's first-ever watertight watch. The Oyster, as the model was christened, gave an impressive demonstration of its waterproof qualities in 1927 when it crossed the English Channel in fifteen and a quarter hours on the wrist of a young English girl swimmer called Mercedes Gleitze. Then, in 1931, Rolex started to market an automatic version of the Oyster; it proved a worldwide success.

The trademark Oyster casing comes in different formats and in different materials and has become the standard-bearer of the Rolex range. The Oyster has been joined by the Datejust, created in 1945 as the first wristwatch to display the date; the Submariner, a model launched in 1953 as the first watch waterproofed to a depth of 100 metres; the 1954 GMT Master, the first automatic water-resistant watch to display dual time zones; the Day Date of 1956, the first model to display in full the days of the week; the Sea-Dweller, whose water-resistant properties were guaranteed to a depth of 610 metres; the Explorer; the Yacht Master; and the Daytona, arguably the most characteristic model in the entire Rolex range, notably in its stainless steel version. Prospective buyers are willing to pay double the asking price for a Daytona simply for the privilege of having the model on their wrist.

Top: *Four versions of the celebrated Daytona Chronograph; the most sought-after is the one in steel with a white dial (shown left).*

Below: *Four variants of the GMT Master with its trademark ancillary 24 hour-graduated magnified time zone display.*

And then there are the older Rolexes, the Rolexes of legend: these are veritable collectors' items and can fetch anything up to £20,000 or $35,000 at auction. The one sported by Paul Newman is the envy of collectors everywhere. Traditionally powered by the equally legendary Zenith El Primero movement, it has been furnished since 2000 with the Cosmograph 4130 movement produced by Rolex entirely in-house, making Rolex a manufactory in its own right …

André J Heiniger took over the helm at Rolex in 1963 and the Rolex myth was perpetuated. The Oyster celebrated its 50th anniversary in 1976. In 1992, Patrick Heiniger was appointed chairman of the Rolex board and it was he who steered the company into the Third Millennium.

It is extremely difficult to obtain detailed information about the brand's finances. Discretion is the watchword in this respect. But it is guesstimated that some seven hundred thousand Rolexes are sold annually worldwide and that close on seven million Rolex movements have been officially recognised as chronometers by the Contrôle Officiel Suisse des Chronomètres.

Irrespective of such data, however, Rolex enjoys and will continue to enjoy iconic status – instantly recognisable and, for many, the ultimate status symbol. The Rolex is a classic or, as they say, *timeless* …

From left to right: *Submariners: steel models from 1953 and from 1959, together with a 1983 Submariner model in steel and gold with date display window.*

dining out in style …

Thursday. Countdown to the weekend. Even if it's back to the office for one more day tomorrow, Thursday evenings are sacred. There are people to meet and things to do. Thursday evenings are ideal for a fine dinner in a high-profile restaurant and perhaps for taking in a nightclub (being careful not to party the night away). All it takes is a couple of phone calls.

A Calvin Klein Challenge Chronograph
in steel, with a rubber bracelet,
a black and red dial with three
secondary dials; quartz-powered
movement with centre-
mounted hour and minute
hands and a date
display window.

What to wear is always an issue. Laid-back and casual, certainly, but not without a deal of thought going into it. After all, an evening on the town has to be taken seriously, especially if a table has been booked at one of the 'in' eateries. To the extent that people are there to see and be seen, designer labels and logos are in order. And that goes for the watch on your wrist …

The rule of thumb is to opt for a super-brand, one that features prominently in all the glossy fashion magazines – a watch that really attracts attention.

Top left: *Célio model in steel with a leather strap and maroon dial; quartz-powered movement with centre-mounted hour, minute and seconds hands.* Right: *A Dior Chiffre Rouge chronograph in steel, with a steel bracelet, silvered dial and three inset counters; automatic movement with centre-mounted hour and minute hands and a date display window.*

Bottom left: *Dolce & Gabbana (D & G) King model with a mock-lizard leather strap and a maroon dial; quartz-powered with centre-mounted hour and minute hands.* Right: *A Chiffre Rouge by Dior: in steel, with a steel bracelet and black dial; automatic movement with centre-mounted hour and minute hands and a date display window.*

This is not to say it should be flamboyant or in poor taste, but it has to pack a punch, to earmark the wearer as one of a select band, the 'happy few', as it were. In these circumstances, clothes and watch should complement each other: the watch must be one hundred per cent geared to fashion.

This is no longer about technology or sophisticated features, this is about *fashion* pure and simple. The sole 'complication' that seems admissible is that the watch should boast a chronograph feature – not because of its intrinsic value but in terms of its overall appearance and *style*.

A Medusa model by Versace, featuring a steel case and bracelet, a black dial, and a quartz-powered movement with centre-mounted hour, minute and seconds hands and a date display window.

A Hydra model
by Façonnable,
with a steel and
rubber bracelet and
a primary dial in brown;
quartz-powered movement
with centre-mounted hour
and minute hands and two
additional time zone displays on
cream-coloured secondary dials.

Gucci Bandeau in steel, with canvas straps and silvered or black dial; Quartz-powered movement with centre-mounted hour and minute hands.

The brand name will be prominently displayed across the dial and perhaps even on the case, rim, strap or clasp. After all, it would be a shame if one were not able to identify the brand at a glance, be it Vuitton, Gucci, Yves Saint Laurent or Versace!

Distinctive motifs and icons are part and parcel of a fashion watch. And the possibilities are limitless: the Medusa motif favoured by Versace, perhaps, or the Gucci Double G, the Lacoste Alligator, the Louis Vuitton monogram or Burberry's tartan.

Lacoste chronograph in steel with a leather strap and black dial with three inset counters; quartz movement with centre-mounted hour and minute hands.

SWISS MADE

*Yves Saint Laurent Rive Gauche
timepiece in steel, with a crocodile
bracelet and a silvered dial; quartz-
powered, with centre-mounted hour
and minute hands.*

Rive Gauche by Yves Saint Laurent: steel, with plaited leather strap and black dial; automatic movement with centre-mounted hour, minute and seconds hands and date display window.

Colour is crucial. Colour changes by brand and by season. Year after year, one signature colour succeeds the previous: some colours are 'in', others are 'out' (only to be back 'in' a couple of years later). Black and white are always and undeniably 'in', but there is an ebb and flow as other colours bow to the dictates of fashion. This is particularly true of dials and straps, where khaki, denim shades and reds feature singly or in combination, either in leather or in fabric. In the case of straps, it is essential for the colour to complement the rest of one's outfit. The 'total look' reigns supreme ...

The number one market for Hong Kong watch exports remains the United States, which in 2004 placed orders to an aggregate value of more than $1.5 billion, 10% up on the previous year.

Preceding double page: *Leading brand sportswear watches worldwide, principally quartz-powered chronographs.*

Page right: *A Boussole (Compass) model by Fendi: steel, with a leather strap and a coloured dial; quartz-powered with hour and minute hands.*

Following double page, page left: *An ST Dupont Géométrie chronograph in steel, with a leather strap and a black dial with three inset counters; quartz-powered, with centre-mounted hour and minute hands and a date display window. Page right: A Heritage model by Burberry: steel casing and bracelet, with silvered tartan-motif dial; quartz-powered with centre-mounted hour, minute and seconds hands and date display window.*

Brand names, logos, motifs, colours – nothing is left to chance. We have come a long way since the production of fashion watches was subcontracted or franchised to firms content to splash a name across the dial and call the product a 'fashion watch': today, the top brands design their own fashion collections under the watchful(!) eye of in-house artistic directors. When the Yves Saint Laurent Collection was launched, for example, it was inconceivable that Tom Ford, then creative director of the PPR Group, which included YSL, Gucci and Boucheron, would not have been one hundred per cent in charge. Ford's involvement effectively legitimised the YSL Collection and his presence at the helm was a guarantee that the celebrated Rive Gauche range embodied the spirit of Yves Saint Laurent himself.

Page right: *Quartz-powered digital model designed by Kenneth Cole: steel, with a leather strap and digital dial.*

Following double page, page left: *Mulberry steel chronograph with leather strap and cream-coloured three-counter dial; quartz-powered, with centre-mounted hour and minute hands and date display window.* Page right: *Steel chronograph by Salvatore Ferragamo, with crocodile bracelet and cream-coloured three-counter dial; quartz-powered with centre-mounted hour, minute and seconds hands and date display window.*

Opposite and page right: *Boss Hugo Boss Maxx Classic in steel with crocodile or steel bracelet and brown dial; automatic movement with centre-mounted hour, minute and seconds hands and a date display window.*

In France, revenue from watch manufacturing is estimated at €382 million.

In 2004, watch production in Hong Kong alone was equivalent to some HK$1.5 billion.

Watches manufactured in Hong Kong and mainland China and exported from Hong Kong in 2004 represented an aggregate value of HK$43.5 billion, 9% up on 2003.

In commercial terms, leading fashion houses have fine-tuned their products to exploit their market potential to the full. Like perfumery, which has proved a valuable adjunct in the case of several fashion houses, watches now generate substantial income. Virtually everyone wears a watch these days, but no one more than the so-called 'fashion victims'. Whether or not they wear watches to tell the time or simply to proclaim their affiliation to some 'in' group or other is, in the final analysis, immaterial. What counts is that these *fashionistas* are addicted to brand names and logos as an integral part of day-to-day living.

Japan turned out
*739 million watches
in 2004, only four million
of which were mechanical.*

Curve by Léonard: steel, with a crocodile bracelet and a black dial; automatic movement with centre-mounted hour, minute and seconds hands and a date display window.

Louis Vuitton, fame in a name

Remarkably, Louis Vuitton made its entry into the watch marketplace only in 2002. The Vuitton brand name is so famous and so international that it comes as a surprise to learn that the firm boasted no dedicated watch range until that year. Vuitton *aficionados* had learned to be patient, however, and their patience was duly rewarded.

There is no place at Louis Vuitton for hit-or-miss design or for short-term marketing solutions. The firm's philosophy is adventurous, but it is also based unequivocally on a permutation of quality and style.

The brand goes back one hundred and fifty years and has remained faithful to the original credo espoused by founder Louis Vuitton. Cabin trunks with the 'LV' logo were an indispensable travel adjunct for the rich and famous, as were monogrammed luggage and accessories meticulously hand-fashioned from top-quality matching and variegated fine leathers and suedes. Vuitton's *prêt-à-porter* range, shoes, jewellery and accessories were all complemented by customised items commissioned by inveterate travellers and collectors alike.

Collector's cabinet with storage room for up to sixteen watches.

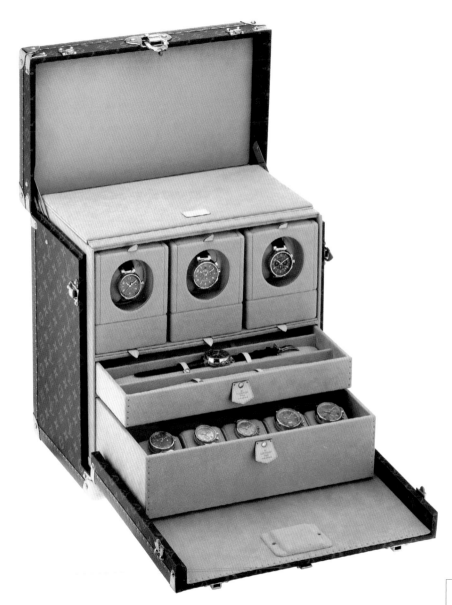

The workshops at Asnières-sur-Seine on the outskirts of Paris are a cornucopia of made-to-measure cases and coffers designed to house such disparate items as fishing tackle, shirts, cigars and even watches. Much of the credit for the initial Louis Vuitton watch range unveiled to the media in Paris in September 2002 must go to the firm's creative director, Marc Jacobs, who had previously masterminded Vuitton's male and female *prêt-à-porter* division. The watch range bears the indelible stamp of Louis Vuitton, not least in terms of quality. The various models feature monogrammed chequerboard casings with the familiar Vuitton canvas shades faithfully reproduced on dials and straps. The hints of gold are an exact match for the gilded elements that featured on the original cabin trunks.

But there is yet more … The Watch Collection is assembled, regulated and quality controlled at the Louis Vuitton workshops in La Chaux-de-Fonds, Switzerland, in proximity to facilities operated by other celebrated watch manufacturers. Each timepiece carries an unconditional five-year warranty.

Page right, left: *Speedy model: steel, with crocodile bracelet and ice-blue dial with three inset counters; automatic movement with centre-mounted hour and minute hands and date display window.* Right: *View of assembly and quality control workshops.*

The watches are quartz-powered or automatic winding, and the complications are trademark Louis Vuitton. In the Tambour and Speedy ranges, for example, there are chronographs, regatta models, divers' watches, twin time-zone models and even a *tourbillon*. Like all other Louis Vuitton products, the Watch Collection is sold exclusively in Vuitton fashion outlets worldwide. There are currently 341 such outlets, 140 of which sell Vuitton watches.

Opposite: *Tambour LV Cup model in steel, with a brown dial with two inset counters and a regatta start countdown feature; automatic movement with centre-mounted hour and minute hands and a date display window.*

Page right: *Tambour diver's watch: steel, with brown dial and rotating lunette inset; automatic movement with centre-mounted hour and minute display, a small seconds hand and a date display window.*

It is well-nigh impossible to estimate how many watches are sold annually, but it can be said with the highest degree of certainty that the Collection has proved an enormous success, judging not only by the number of watches flaunted on wrists but also by the long queues outside Vuitton boutiques. The Louis Vuitton Boutique on the Champs Elysées in Paris is now a landmark monument in the French capital, attracting as many visitors annually as the Eiffel Tower …

Left: *A Tambour tourbillon in pink gold with a transparent sapphire dial and a galuchat (shark-skin) strap; mechanically wound movement with centre-mounted hour and minute hands.*

Right: *Tambour chronograph in steel with a brown dial and three inset counters; automatic movement with centre-mounted hour and minute hands and a date display window.*

party time …

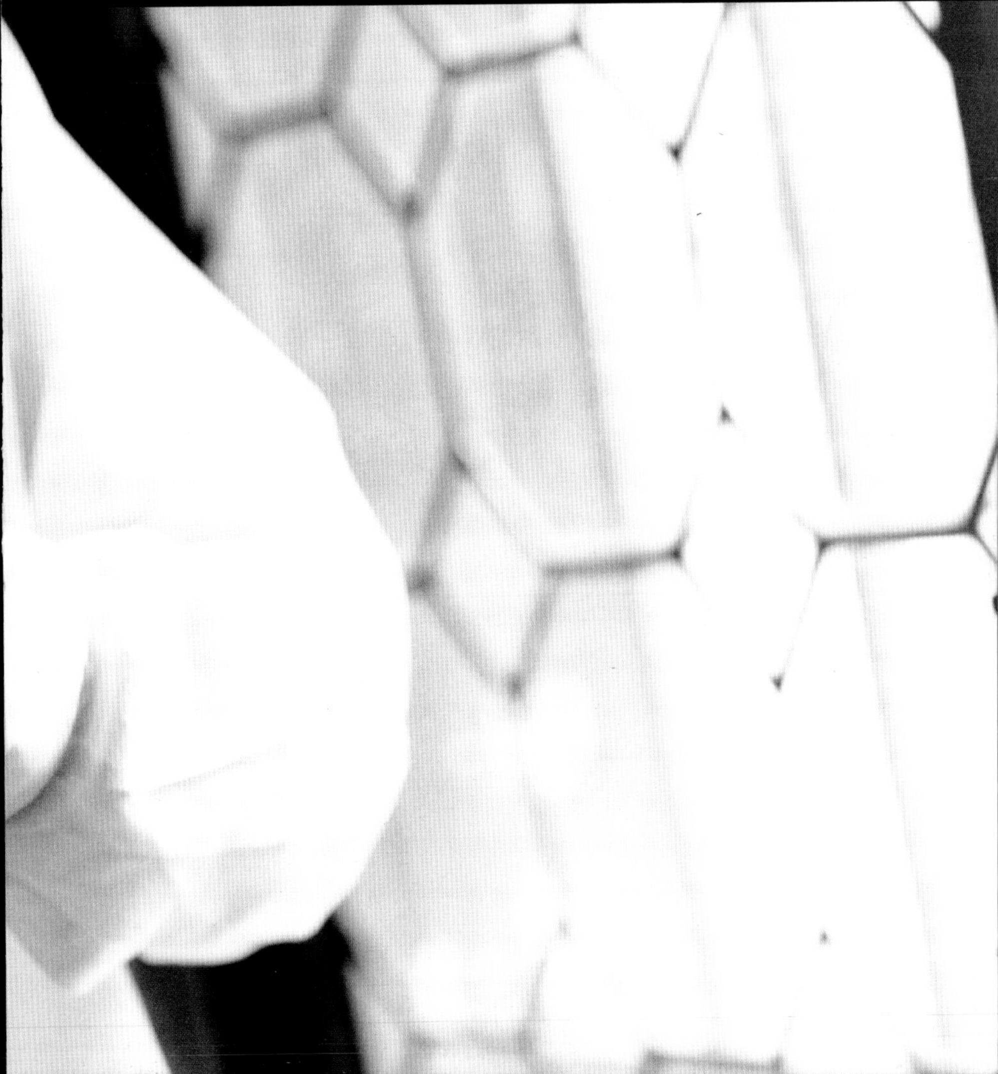

The standard working week is over and it's leisure time again. Time passes so quickly these days that it's hard to believe that the weekend has come around once more. Staid work clothes are consigned to the wardrobe and out comes the evening finery. It's time to have some fun …

Once again, dressing up for a formal occasion implies choosing a watch that fits the bill. A dress watch is one thing, but this calls for something more elegant, more sophisticated.

Page right: Chaumet Dandy: white gold with a satin strap, the perfect complement to formal evening wear …

What, exactly, remains to be seen, but a dress watch-plus is indicated: something simple, of course, something ultra-thin with an enamelled face, perhaps, or even mother-of-pearl? Best might be a plain white face with a *soupçon* of silver, and a black surround or, failing that, dark blue or anthracite grey. The watch case should ideally be in white, yellow or possibly pink gold, and two-tone or platinum would be even better. The whole to be set off by a simple saddle-stitched black strap (hardly ever maroon) or a matt or glossy alligator strap. There you have it: a thumbnail sketch of elegance as perceived by a watch fanatic. In terms of sophistication, the accent is not so much on originality as on rarity value and impact. Let's face it, above all an evening timepiece has to be *chic* …

Piaget's 'Altiplano XL': white gold, with crocodile bracelet and silvered dial; ultra-slim manually-wound movement with centre-mounted hour and minute hands.

The world's smallest mechanically adjustable winding mechanism features in the Jaeger-leCoultre Caliber 101 of 1929. The total volume of the 3.4 mm (1/8 in) thick rectangular mechanism is 0.2 cm^3, and the weight amounts to less than one gram.

Geneva is the undisputed capital of the watch world. The city plays host not only to the headquarter operations of the most prestigious brands but also to the world's major watch auctions, whose 2004 total turnover came to nearly SFr95 million.

Opposite: *Hermès assembly in yellow gold, with crocodile bracelet and yellow gold dial; automatic movement with centre-mounted hour, minute and seconds hands and a date display window.*

Page left, top: *Monsieur Arpels from Van Cleef & Arpels: steel, with crocodile bracelet and black onyx dial; manually wound movement with eccentric hour and minute hands and a small seconds hand at bottom centre. A perpetual dateline features on the reverse.* Below: *Ultra-slim model in white gold with crocodile bracelet and white dial; manually wound ultra-slim movement with centre-mounted hour and minute hands (Jaeger-leCoultre).*

A straightforward round or square-faced watch meets the criteria for elegance, but real sophistication typically comes in the form of an ultra-thin movement. In the great majority of cases, the movement will be mechanical and hand-wound or, at worst, automatic. There is nothing particularly sophisticated about a quartz watch, and that variant is admissible provided only that the case is genuinely elegant. In other words, exceptions *can* be made, but the golden rule is to stick with something mechanical. Lapses in taste are frowned upon on an evening such as this ...

The world's most linear movement *was launched in its original version by Corum in 1980. In its most recent reincarnation, elaborated in conjunction with the Vaucher manufactory, the hand-wound, baguette-shaped movement is a mere 3 mm (1/8 in) thick and 4.9 mm (1/5 in) long; it is used to power Corum's new Golden Bridge model range.*

Breguet Classique in yellow gold, with crocodile bracelet and guilloché dial; manually wound movement with centre-mounted hour and minute hands.

Ultra-thin mechanical movements are available from a wide range of manufacturers, but Piaget has made wafer-thin models its speciality. Piaget hit the headlines in 1956, when the firm unveiled its Calibre 9P, a revolutionary model inasmuch as it housed the thinnest mechanical movement ever. The 9P was a legend in its own right and, when revamped and re-christened the 430P in 1996, it retained its ultra-flat credentials to the millimetre, despite the intervening years: 2.1 mm (1/12 in) thin and 20.5 mm (4/5 in) in diameter. A dream watch …

Piaget was understandably proud of its offspring and used it as a template for an entire catalogue range. Today, other commercially available extra-flat watches boast similar dimensions – and there are a relatively high number of ultra-thin styles now on offer.

Altiplano by Piaget: white gold, crocodile bracelet and black dial; ultra-slim manually wound movement with centre-mounted hour and minute hands.

Opposite: *Platinum Altiplano by Piaget, with crocodile bracelet and copper dial; ultra-slim manually wound movement with centre-mounted hour and minute hands.*

PIAGET

SWISS MADE

Page right: *The LUC Twist by Chopard: steel, with crocodile bracelet and two-tone black-and-white dial; automatic movement with centre-mounted hour and minute hands, a small seconds hand and a date display window.*

When it is said that a company 'manufactures' a brand, it means that it produces virtually all of the requisite components but also at least one of the movements incorporated into the watch.

Antiquorum, the specialist watch industry auction house, was launched by Osvaldo Patrizzi a mere 30 years ago, but is the acknowledged market leader, with a 2004 turnover totalling more than SFr105 million.

Opposite: *Classic Gent
by Ebel: gold and steel,
crocodile bracelet and
white dial; quartz-
powered with centre-
mounted hour, minute
and seconds hands and
a date display window.*

Page left:
*Franck Muller's
Casablanca: platinum,
with a leather bracelet and
a grey dial; automatic movement
with centre-mounted hour, minute and
seconds hands and date display window.*

party time ...

The thinnest movement in the world is the ETA 599.001, which powers the ultra-thin Skin model developed by Swatch in 1992 and commercially available from 1997. The watch casing and movement together are a remarkable 3.9 mm (1/6 in) thin and have a combined weight of only 12.3 g (less than 1/2 ounce).

Page left: *Chaumet Dandy in pink gold, with satin strap and black dial; manually wound movement with centre-mounted hour and minute hands and a small seconds hand.*

Opposite: *Hermès assembly in platinum, with crocodile bracelet and enamel dial; automatic movement with centre-mounted hour, minute and seconds hands and a date display window.*

party time …

Although the British watch industry has almost disappeared, there are stylish watches with British brand names such as Storm and RLT, assembled in Britain and mostly using Swiss or Japanese movements.

French watch exports are estimated at €246 million. The leading export destination is Switzerland, followed by Japan and the United States.

Vacheron Constantin's Patrimony model in yellow gold, with crocodile bracelet and enamel dial; automatic movement with trailing hour and minute hands.

Ultra-thinness may be one yardstick of sophistication, but other features of the dress watch-plus must be original and leading-edge. Here, we enter a whole new world of watch design, a world dominated by exceptional creativity in conjunction with hitherto unimaginable technological expertise. Watch design has moved up a dimension to a point most people would scarcely credit. Thus, dials are adorned with *cloisonné* enamel art miniatures, genuinely 'new' Old Masters re-created on a basis of innumerable coats of enamel, each fired and polished in turn. Colours are marked off, one from the other, by means of gold-thread filaments inserted painstakingly by hand.

Avenue C by Harry Winston:
platinum, with crocodile bracelet and
ruthenium and silver dial; manually
wound movement with flyback
features and seconds hand.

Blancpain's Villeret: white gold,
with crocodile bracelet and
silvered opaline dial; ultra-slim
automatic movement with centre-
mounted hour and minute hands
and power reserve indicator.

Grand Osmior by L Leroy: yellow gold, with crocodile bracelet, silvered guilloché dial; ultra-slim manually wound movement with centre-mounted hour and minute hands.

Other astonishing examples include cases fashioned entirely from rock crystal, where the privileged wearer has the sensation of a watch 'suspended' on his wrist, with the movements appearing to emanate from the core of a perfectly polished crystal block. The most recent creation in this category is the Golden Bridge, the most linear movement in the world, developed by the Corum Manufactory in 1980. An updated version has now been produced in tandem with the Vaucher Manufactory located in Fleurier in the Swiss Jura. This hand-wound, *baguette*-shaped watch is a striking 3 mm (1/8 in) thin and is 4.9 mm (1/5 in) long – yet another marvel of design.

Whether ultra-thin, *cloisonné*-enamelled or fashioned from rock crystal, however, any evening dress watch worthy of the name will project an aura of sophistication and will stand out from those around it. This is male jewellery at its most consummate, something that will grace any formal occasion.

Corum's Golden Bridge: pink gold, with crocodile bracelet and transparent sapphire dial; manually wound movement with centre-mounted hour and minute hands.

François-Paul Journe, making his mark

François-Paul Journe is French, young and exceptionally talented. Without doubt, he personifies all that is good in contemporary watchmaking. As one might anticipate, models signed by Journe are today among the most coveted on the planet.

François-Paul Journe's career is best described as atypical. This new star in the watchmaking firmament is today widely acknowledged as the spiritual heir of the legendary Abraham-Louis Breguet (the 'father' of high-end watchmaking). Journe studied initially at La Perrine, the watch school in Marseille, before transferring to Paris to complete his studies in 1976. Journe learned the delicate art of watch restoration with his uncle, working on antique pieces that he repaired and reassembled – much to the delight of a rapidly expanding clientele. Journe's uncle was one of the few front-rank watchmakers in Paris at the time and, as a result, had a whole string of well-heeled collectors among his customers. François-Paul was as committed as he was talented, the upshot being that he rapidly made his mark. His first own-design watch, dating from 1982, featured a *tourbillon* and was exhibited at the Musée de l'Horlogerie in La Chaux-de-Fonds.

François-Paul Journe and his workshop in Geneva.

F.P.JOURNE
Invenit et fecit

Tourbillon Souverain (Sovereign):
platinum, with platinum bracelet
and rhodié gold dial; manually wound
movement with eccentric hour and minute
hands and a small seconds hand.

Platinum Octa
Chronograph with
crocodile bracelet,
rhodié gold dial and three
inset counters; automatic
movement with eccentric hour
and minute hands, a small seconds
hand at centre left, a date display
window and a flyback feature.

Resonance chronograph: platinum, with crocodile bracelet and rhodié gold dial; manually wound movement with dual display for hours, minutes and seconds and a power reserve indicator.

Three years later, in 1985, François-Paul Journe struck out on his own, setting up his own *atelier* in the Rue de Verneuil. When his uncle retired, François-Paul inherited many of the latter's clients. He continued to do restoration and repair work, but also started to work on individual commissions to design one-off models. The first watches carrying his signature did the rounds of major collectors and his reputation was soon made. In 1995, Journe decided it was time to move to Geneva. From then on, he collaborated with various manufactories and, as of 1998, began work on his first-ever collection. This was exhibited at the 1999 Basel Fair and François-Paul Journe was up and running with a vengeance: in his first year, he sold 50 watches, in his second, 105, followed by 180, 250, then 350, and so on. In 2003, Journe bought the building in the heart of Geneva which now serves as his manufactory, a 2,000m^2 facility that has all the hallmarks of a 21st-century watchmaking plant, with wholly vertically integrated production and quality control processes. Today, François-Paul Journe employs some fifty co-workers and turns out around seven hundred timepieces annually. His collections feature models with *tourbillons*, chronographs, power reserve indicators, moon-phase displays and so on. His watches are exclusively mechanical and each gold or platinum piece is unique. François-Paul Journe's talent is singular and exceptional: his elegant, sophisticated and original creations are such that he is widely respected as the *doyen* of formal watch design.

Octa in red gold, with crocodile bracelet and red gold dial; automatic movement in solid red gold with eccentric hour, minute and seconds display, a date display window and a power reserve indicator.

un and games …

It's a beautiful morning, the gang are already in town and there's not a minute to lose. So head for the garage and roll out the vintage automobile for a day's drive along country lanes in the company of one's peers. The engine is running like a dream, the coachwork is polished, tyre pressures are checked, driving gloves donned and sunglasses adjusted. All that remains now is to get behind the wheel and leave the congested city traffic far behind. Aren't we forgetting something? A suitable watch, perhaps?

Mercedes-Benz Calendar with leather strap and silvered dial; automatic movement with centre-mounted hour, minute and seconds display, power reserve indicator, day-of-the-week pointer, and week number and date display window.

fun and games ...

Once again, the range and diversity of today's watches is plain for all to see – nowhere more perhaps than in the automotive world, which has been a constant source of inspiration. Hardly surprising, of course, because there are striking similarities between a watch dial and an instrument panel, notably the format (generally round) and the needles used to display speed, revs and the like … But the similarities don't end there. A passion for cars often goes hand in hand with a passion for watches, top-of-the-range footwear and fine cigars. Why else would prestige car manufacturers exhibiting at motor show's instruct their stand hostesses to check a would-be buyer's watch before admitting him to the stand? If he is wearing a superb watch, chances are that he will not only have a taste for the Porsche lifestyle but also the wherewithal to pay for it.

Preceding double page: *TAG Heuer unveiled its SLR Automatic Chronograph to coincide with the launch of the luxurious Mercedes-Benz SLR McLaren.*

Page right: *Omega's Speedmaster Michael Schuhmacher: The Legend, a steel-case chronograph with a steel bracelet, red dial and three inset black counters; automatic movement with centre-mounted hour and minute hands and a date display window.*

Today's watch designers draw inspiration from the automotive sector and it is significant that the two sectors are increasingly linked in the public's imagination. Watch manufacturers make their presence felt as sponsors by advertising their wares on Grand Prix circuits and elsewhere, and there are a number of household-name drivers who have cooperated with watch firms to provide input to watch design. From time to time, car manufacturers even get together to develop a common design range. Hedonistic? Certainly. But isn't that what we're all about?

Lancel's Chronographe Classique: steel, with a perforated leather strap, a black and silvered dial and three inset counters; quartz-powered with centre-mounted hour and minute displays and a date window.

Page right: Dunhill's Carwatch: pink gold and high tech ceramics, with a leather strap and a black dial; automatic movement with centre-mounted hour, minute and seconds hands and a date display window.

Page left: *Girard-Perregaux's Tribute: a tourbillon dedicated to Enzo Ferrari. Fashioned from platinum, with a crocodile bracelet and a black dial. The manually wound movement features chronograph functions and a perpetual dateline display.*

Below: *A Gérard Charles-design Turbo chronograph in black steel, with a crocodile bracelet and a black dial with three inset counters; automatic movement with centre-mounted hour and minute functions and date display window.*

AUDEMARS PIGUET
MILLENARY
MASERATI
MASERATI
ANNIVERSARY
90
LIMITED EDITION

vodafone
AUDEMARS PIGUET
AP
BOSCH
PIRELLI
WWW.MASERATI.COM

Page left and opposite: Audemars-Piguet produced a limited series of 450 pieces in celebration of Maserati's 90th anniversary. The watch in question was a version of the Millenary, fashioned in pink gold, with an automatic movement powering hour and minute hands, a secondary time zone function, a power reserve indicator, a date display and a day-night feature.

Contemporary watch designers go well beyond the simple incorporation of automotive elements into their watch and strap designs, as is the case with Lancel, Dunhill or Gérald Charles. When a watch firm elects to sponsor a particular event, for example, it will often launch a commemorative model, as was the case with Chopard and its Mille Miglia chronographs issued annually to mark the famous rally event in Italy.

Opposite: *Chopard's Mille Miglia GMT 2005 Chronograph has a rubber bracelet with a tyre motif and a white dial with three black counters; automatic movement with centre-mounted hour and minute functions, a date display window and an alternate time zone feature distinguished by a pointer on a 24-hour engraved central lunette. The piece was in yellow gold and released in a limited series of 250.* Page right: *A steel variant was issued in a limited series of 2005 units.*

Page left: *Chopard's limited
series (500 units) Mille Miglia
GMT Alfa Romeo 6C 1750 GS,
featuring a steel case, a printed tyre
motif rubber bracelet and a black dial with
three counters. The automatic movement has centre-
mounted hour and minute functions, a date display
window and a secondary time zone display in the form
of a pointer on a 24-hour engraved central lunette.*

Also shown: *a 1910 Barrett-Jackson watch in steel,
with a natural rubber bracelet and a pearl motif dial;
automatic movement with centre-mounted hour,
minute and seconds hands, plus a date display porthole.*

As far as drivers and watch brands are concerned, one need look no further than the collaboration between Omega and Michael Schuhmacher. 'Schumi' has been part of the 'Dream Team' for several years; in 2005, when Omega launched its three-model collection entitled The Legend to mark his string of Formula 1 championship successes, there could scarcely have been a more fitting accolade. But this was actually nothing new. When screen actor Steve McQueen wore a TAG Heuer watch on the set of *Le Mans* in 1971, TAG Heuer promptly contributed to automotive mythology by bringing out the Monaco, an updated version of the model worn in the film *(see page 96)*.

Page right: *A Van Der Bauwede-designed Magnum GT Modena chronograph in steel, with a perforated leather strap and a white dial with three counters; quartz-powered, with centre-mounted hour and minute functions and a date display window.*

Following double-page: *The titanium Ingénieur (Engineer) is a joint production by IWC and Mercedes AMG. The strap is in Kevlar®. Automatic movement with centre-mounted hour, minute and seconds hands and a date display function.*

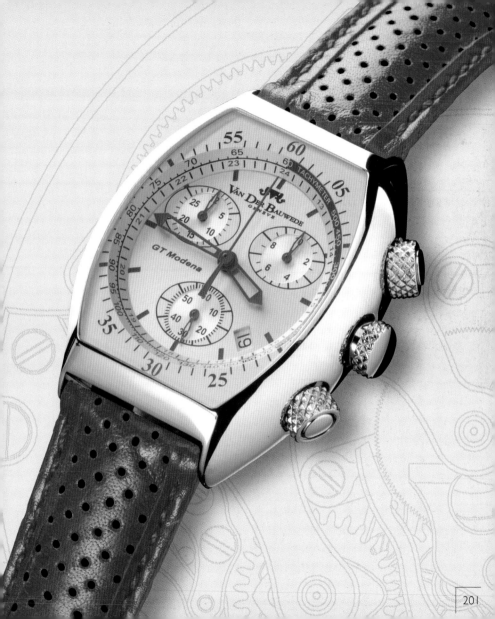

fun and games ...

The love story between automotive manufacturers and watch firms is in evidence elsewhere and the list of happy marriages is too long to be reproduced in the present context. Suffice it to say that successful pairings have included Audemars Piguet and Maserati, Girard-Perregaux and Ferrari, IWC and Mercedes AMG, Oris and Formula I stable BMW Williams, Parmigiani Fleurier and Bugatti, Breitling and Bentley, Frédérique Constant and Austin Healey, Jaeger-leCoultre and Aston Martin, and so on. 'Tie-ins' like these are meat and drink to automobile fans who typically sport watches with legendary logos and motifs that correspond to their favourite automobile marques.

Watches are now regarded as a viable investment option – *the total revenue from the sale of collectors' items doubled in 2004, increasing from £47 million to £94 million ($86 million to $172 million).*

Breitling designed this pink gold tourbillon chronograph for automotive manufacturer Bentley.

Jaeger-leCoultre's Memovox Aston Martin: steel, with a leather strap and a black dial; automatic movement with centre-mounted hour, minute and seconds functions and a date display window.

Chronoris Chronograph by Oris: steel case, with perforated leather strap, black and orange dial and counter inset. The automatic movement powers centre-mounted hour and minute functions and a date display window.

Swiss watch exports posted their best-ever results in 2004, with over SFr10.5 billion in revenue from the sale of more than 25 million units.

The LVMH Group's total net profits exceeded one billion euros in 2004. Its watchmaking arm posted an operational profit of €13 million in 2004 following a €48 million deficit in the previous year.

Watch cases mirror alloy wheel designs, dials are manufactured in Formula 1 bodywork carbon or in metal with a raised finish reminiscent of ancient fascias, complication sub-dials are in the style of rev counters, hour and minute hands are hollowed out like steering wheel struts, and natural rubber wriststraps mimic automotive tyres. Total synthesis …

Parmigiani Fleurier launched its Bugatti Type 370 to coincide with the long-awaited unveiling of the new Bugatti Veyron EB 16.4. The white gold piece exhibits an unconventional design, with a manually wound transverse movement and hours and minutes recorded on the casing profile. The movement is visible through the transparent sapphire face.

Porsche Design, marque of authenticity

Not to put too fine a point on it: Porsche is to cars as Rolex is to watches. Both have attained mythical status. So, when an institution of the stature of Porsche goes into the watch business, its models have the indelible stamp of authenticity. Ferdinand Porsche was born in December 1935 and was obsessed with design from a very early age. He attended the college of art and design in Ulm, then entered the family business, where he worked on coachwork and engine prototype design. Some years later, he was appointed to the post of chief designer and in 1962 he unveiled the Porsche 904 and the Porsche 911. In 1972, after his nomination to the Porsche board of directors, he founded Porsche Design, based in Stuttgart, his objective being to pursue his personal design ambitions in various fields. Above all, he was able to indulge his second great love: watches.

Page right, below: *Ferdinand Porsche*. Above and right: *Rear and profile views of the black-coated titanium Indicator, the first automatic chronograph to display elapsed times numerically.*

Following double page, left: *Ferdinand Porsche was the originator of the Porsche 911*. Right: *The Indicator: black-coated titanium with rubber bracelet and black guilloché dial. The automatic movement features a centre-mounted hour, minute and chronograph pointer, a small seconds hand at left centre, a power reserve indicator at bottom centre and windows which display elapsed times.*

The first item to figure in the Porsche Watch Design catalogue was a completely black chronograph inspired by the fascia design of the Porsche 911. The watch was launched in 1974 and some fifty thousand units were sold virtually overnight to sports car enthusiasts and watch aficionados. Porsche Watch Design continued to make inroads into the market until 1995, when Porsche acquired Eterna, a leading Swiss watch manufacturer noted for the first-ever alarm watch (1914) and for its patented automatic watch winding mechanism based on ball-bearings: the Eterna-Matic system.

All Porsche Design timepieces are now developed and produced at the Eterna workshops in Switzerland and the 'Swiss Made' quality label features on every Porsche watch dial. Porsche Design models are regarded as the most authentic 'drivers' watches' in the marketplace thanks to this unique combination of Porsche's reputation as an automotive manufacturer and Eterna's status as one of the standard-bearers of traditional Swiss watchmaking craftsmanship. Porsche Design watches come in a range of shapes and forms, ranging from the simple to the complex.

Models are in quartz or automatic winding format, fashioned from stainless steel or titanium and mounted on metal or rubber wriststraps.

The Porsche dial display is above all highly readable and ergonomic – as one might expect from designers who have created instrument panels for high-performance sports cars.

The Porsche Design range includes expensive and complex timepieces such as the P 6613 Chronograph, in pink gold and with a fly-back hand, together with resolutely sporty items such as the Indicator, the first automatically winding chronograph to display times in digital format. This feature is a favourite of Porsche's new CEO, Ernst Seyr, who admits to being a devotee of all things mechanical. Before becoming involved with Porsche

Watch Seyr was better known as the designer behind the celebrated Katana light aircraft.

Below: Ernst Seyr, CEO of Eterna Porsche Design, seen here introducing the Indicator at the Basel Fair.

Page right: Flyback Chronograph in pink gold, with crocodile bracelet and a black dial with four inset counters; automatic movement with centre-mounted hour and minute functions and date indicator.

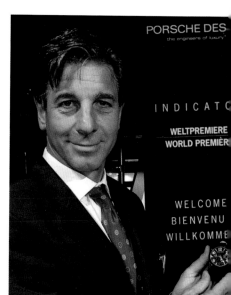

SUNDAY, 10 A.M.

this sporting life …

Morning in the city and a beautiful day in prospect. No excuse for not making the best of it. Today is going to be devoted to sport. There's nothing like a bit of physical exercise to recharge the batteries for the week ahead. One of the great things about the weekend is the fact that you can take things at your own pace. Seconds, minutes, quarters of an hour drift by and, before you know it, another hour has passed. The sun is up, the sky is blue and it's ten o' clock already. Time to get the show on the road …

Jaeger-leCoultre's Master Compressor chronograph in steel, with leather strap and black dial with three counters; automatic movement with centre-mounted hour and minute functions and date display window.

It's also time to put Saturday's legendary pairings – Reverso Aston Martin, Breitling Bentley, Chopard Mille Miglia and such – back in their box. Today is chronograph day.

When it comes to chronographs, the choice is extensive. As our after-office drink on Tuesday established (see page 62), the chronograph is the most common of all watch complications, not to say the most useful and the most accessible. This explains why chronographs have come to dominate the watch landscape to such a degree.

The world's most accurate (and most celebrated) automatic chronograph is El Primero, designed by Zenith in 1969. It was, and still is, the sole automatic movement capable of measuring in units of 0.1 of a second.

Chaumet's Class One XL chronograph in pink gold, with rubber bracelet and black guilloché dial with three inset counters; quartz-powered with centre-mounted hour and minute functions and a date display window.

220

Opposite:
Bvlgari's Assioma: steel chronograph with a steel bracelet and a grey dial with three inset counters; automatic movement with centre-mounted hour and date functions and a date display window.

Page right: *The Bell & Ross Instrument BR 01 chronograph: steel, with leather strap and black dial with three inset counters; automatic movement with centre-mounted hour and minute functions and a date display window.*

this sporting life ...

Article 1a of the 'Swiss Made' regulation, deems a watch to be of Swiss manufacture if at least 50% of the movement components are of Swiss origin, if it was assembled and encased in Switzerland and if final quality control was effected in Switzerland.

Page left and opposite:
Roadstar chronographs by Cartier: steel, with leather strap or steel bracelet and a brown dial with three inset counters; automatic movement with centre-mounted hour and minute functions and a date display window.

Chronographs come in various shapes and sizes and have a tendency to run in groups. First off, there are formal chronographs – namely those designated as such by the manufacturer. Then there are those that have a more sporty look. Finally, there are those that are deliberately sport-oriented to the extent that they are totally geared to competition.

Chronographs are handy to have around on a day-to-day basis – they are useful when it comes to boiling a three-minute egg, as the saying goes – but they really come into their own in a sporting context, where they are indispensable in terms of measuring one's performance (and boosting one's ego). Besides, they are much more bulky and, in consequence, substantially more impressive than a conventional watch with its modest contingent of two or three hands. A chronograph is there to be *noticed*, to send out a *signal*. Let's face it: how many men are there who have never played a day's sport in their lives yet still brandish a whopping great Rolex or Breitling on their wrist as an apparent token of their athletic prowess and a symbol of their virility?

When a watch manufacturer refers to a chronograph, however, the emphasis is not on sport but simply on a specific feature or complication. The chronograph is no more and no less than an attractive additional feature on a hand-wound (but more often than not automatic) watch, a complication that appeals to watch aficionados. The chronograph may be in pink, yellow or grey gold or even in platinum, with an elegant saddle-stitch alligator strap.

Despite the exorbitant prices that some timepieces attract, the average price of a watch is under £10 …

It is estimated that the annual total worldwide sale of watches stands at 1.5 billion units.

The aggregate value of the world watch market is currently estimated at £30 billion ($55 billion).

Preceding page: *Montblanc's Summit chronograph: steel, with lizard-skin bracelet and brown dial with three counters; quartz-powered, with centre-mounted hour and minute functions and a date display window.*

Opposite: *Olympic chronograph by Longines: steel, with crocodile bracelet and beige-coloured dial with two counters; automatic movement with centre-mounted hour and minute functions and a date display window.*

At its most basic, the chronograph complication involves incorporating three sub-dials (a 30-minute counter, a 12-hour counter and a second-hand counter) grouped around a central timing hand. Start, stop and reset functions are commanded by means of depressing and releasing twin buttons mounted on either side of the standard winding stem. In purely watchmaking terms, that is all there is to it.

Needless to say, however, manufacturers have come up with all manner of variants. Sometimes there are only two sub-dials (on models from the 1950s, for example, which now fetch record prices at auction) and the two auxiliary buttons are dispensed with, so that only the crown on the winder stem is required to activate the chronograph function. And – once again in purely watchmaking terms – manufacturers have not hesitated to build in other complications, such as twin time zones or a perpetual calendar.

The Longines Olympic chronograph: steel, with steel bracelet and a black dial with two counters; automatic movement with centre-mounted hour and minute functions and a date display window.

this sporting life …

Page left and opposite:
Chanel's J12 chronograph,
black or white high tech ceramic,
with matching black or white
high tech ceramic bracelets,
and black or white dials with
three inset counters; automatic
movement with centre-mounted
hour and minute functions and a
date display window.

In such cases, the so-called chronograph emerges as an exceptional collector's item and is light years away from the Sunday morning models used simply to record lap times.

Next, there are chronographs that have a sporty look. They may be automatic or quartz-driven, but they will inevitably be deliberately bulky (up to 40 mm [1 1/2 in] in diameter). The automatic variant will feature an anti-shock function, whereas this is superfluous in quartz models. There will be three sub-dials to afford heightened legibility and there will typically be two auxiliary command buttons for ease of use. Most will be made from stainless steel and will feature water-repellent straps in stainless steel or rubber.

Baume & Mercier steel chronograph with rubber bracelet and a black dial with three inset silvered counters; automatic movement with centre-mounted hour and minute hands and a date display window.

this sporting life ...

These sports chronographs may also be fashioned from lightweight titanium, a material that is not only durable but is also known for its non-allergic properties. This latter type belongs very much in the status symbol category: flashy, relatively expensive and 'in-your-face' enough to convey an impression of wealth and virility – particularly popular in the case of non-sporty types desperate for recognition. The out-and-out sports chronograph, on the other hand, will be quartz-driven (more robust than the mechanical variant) and will be impervious to water, shocks and sudden movements. These chronographs are equally at home on a ski-slope, during a marathon, in a paragliding context or, quite simply, anywhere where sudden and violent movement may be anticipated.

Preceding double page, left: *The TAG Heuer Autavia chronograph: steel, with steel bracelet and black dial with two inset counters; automatic movement with centre-mounted hour and minute functions and date display window. The winder is situated on the left of the casing.* Right: *The Omega Speedmaster Professional: steel, with steel bracelet and blue dial with three inset counters; manually wound movement with centre-mounted hour, minute and seconds functions.*

Page right: *Kronotype's Chronograph VI: titanium, with crocodile bracelet, white and grey dial and three inset counters; automatic movement with centre-mounted hour and minute functions.*

this sporting life ...

The first watch with two hands was produced in 1691 by Dutch physicist, astronomer and surveyor Christian Huyghens.

The quartz watch premiered in 1967. Known as the Beta 21, it was developed by the Neuchâtel-based Research Centre for Electronic Horology.

Page left: *Hublot chronograph Super B: steel, with natural rubber bracelet and brown dial with three inset counters; automatic movement with centre-mounted hour and minute functions and a date display window.*

Opposite: *The Dolce Vita Gran Turismo by Longines: steel, leather strap, white guilloché dial with three inset counters; quartz-powered with centre-mounted hour and minute functions and a date display window.*

Left and right: *Quartz-powered
Swatch chronographs in plastic.*

Above: Three chronographs from the Seiko Sportura range. The model on the left is powered by an automatic 'Kinetic' movement which affords quartz-like precision.

To the extent that they are electronic, all manner of additional functions can be miniaturised and incorporated. Thus, in addition to the 'standard' chronometric function, they can be fitted out with a thermometer, an altimeter, a compass, a heart-rate monitor or a memory archive (Casio even has a complication that measures tide coefficients). In sum, this type of chronograph marks a radical departure from the traditional concept of a 'watch' and is more akin to an onboard computer. In terms of design, these extreme sports models are best described as 'futuristic' – in the sense that they may have dual analogue/digital dials, electro-luminous liquid crystal displays, and integrated casing and bracelets. They can be fashioned from high-tensile strength polymers, rubber, bonded steel and aluminium, and so on.

Watch aficionados wear these models when indulging in their favourite sport. The younger generation, meanwhile, simply adores the intrinsic gadgetry and can reel off by heart the names of the leading brands …

The first G-Shock launched by Casio in 1983 revolutionised mechanical chronography: an ultra-resistant multi-function electronic timepiece, it quickly made its mark in the field of extreme sports.

Steel chronograph by
Fred, with steel and
rubber bracelet and
a black and grey dial
with three counters;
quartz-powered, with
centre-mounted hour
and minute display and
a date display window.

Aquanautic chronograph model: steel, with steel and rubber bracelet and black dial with three inset counters; automatic movement with centre-mounted hour and minute display and a date display window.

Casio, from pipes to watches

The Casio brand is today an icon of the Asian watch industry and it has built a universal reputation on the strength of its track record as an innovator and 'miniaturiser' ever since the end of World War II. How this came about is astonishing.

At the end of World War II, Japan's economy was in dire straits. The tobacco industry continued to flourish, however, because the Japanese were, at the time, a nation of heavy smokers. One of the Kashio brothers spotted a market opportunity and came up with an unusual idea: a cross between a pipe and a cigarette-holder that could be slipped over a finger like a normal ring.

The ring-pipe device meant that a cigarette could be smoked down to the very last flake of tobacco. It was a runaway success and, by 1946, the Kashio family had struck it rich. Engineer Tadio Kashio went on to set up the Kashio Seisakujo Company in Tokyo and started producing calculators. His initial prototype was unveiled in 1954 and weighed in at a staggering 140 kg (22 stone) – more like a large dining table than a hand-held device.

Spearheaded today by Kazuo Kashio (below, right), watchmaker Casio made its debut in Japan in 1946 under the brandname Kashio Seisakujo (top). The first calculator prototype was launched in 1954 (below, left) and weighed in at 140 kg (22 stone) – a far cry from today's miniaturised versions.

Over time, however, calculator design was streamlined and dimensions were progressively reduced until, in 1957, the first 'compact' electronic calculator came on to the market. At this juncture, Casio Computer & Co, Ltd was formed and, by 1966, Casio calculators were being exported to the four corners of the globe. By the following year, Casio had subsidiaries all over the world. The first genuine hand-held calculator as we know it today went on sale to the general public in 1972. It proved an overwhelming success. It was then that Casio decided to diversify into watches, doing so with a vengeance: its quartz-based models proved so revolutionary that the mechanical watch industry in Switzerland was so badly hit that it practically imploded. In 1974, the firm's Casiotron made its debut as the first fully automated watch offering a digital display not only of the hours, minutes and seconds but also of the month, date and day of the week. Further revolutionary models came thick and fast. The first G-Shock was launched in 1983 and is still the firm's best-selling model. It is billed as 'ultra-resistant' and fully lives up to that term, being capable of surviving unscathed when dropped from the top of a building to the pavement below. The G-Shock is a multi-function watch with a signature chronograph feature that rivals its mechanical counterparts in terms of accuracy.

Top left: *1957: First compact electric calculator.*

Top right: *1972: First modern hand-held calculator.*

Bottom left: *1974: Casio's first watch, christened the 'Casiotron'.*

Bottom right: *2002: The first solar energy-powered G-Shock.*

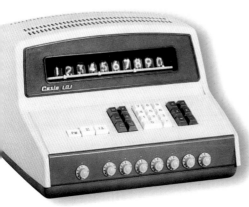

Thanks to quartz technology, the chronograph has a built-in memory mode. As such, the Casio-style chronograph is effectively ahead of its time and would not be out of place in a sci-fi scenario set in the year 2025 …

1984 saw the advent of the first Casio watch capable of memorising telephone numbers. This was followed in 1985 by the first ultra-thin (just 3.9 mm [1/5 in] thick) digital model, then by the first barometer-watch (1989), the first GPS (1999), the first camera-watch (2000) and, in 2001, by the first solar energy-powered 'atomic' watch.

Over the years, Casio's G-Shock has continued to develop, to the delight of the firm's current president and CEO, Kazua Kashio. The G-Shock is a monument to innovation in the world watch industry and is synonymous with the quartz chronograph. 'We shall continue to innovate,' promises Kazua Kashio, 'as long as we can bring pleasure to people everywhere'.

A bold undertaking indeed …

Top left: *1989: First digital watch equipped with a barometer.*

Top right: *1984: First watch with telephone number storage capability.*

Bottom left: *1999: First watch with GPS capability.*

Bottom right: *2000: First watch with in-built camera function.*

contact information

Audemars Piguet,
www.audemarspiguet.com
Auguste Reymond, www.augus-
tereymond.ch
Bell & Ross, www.bellross.com
Blancpain, www.blancpain.com
Breguet, www.breguet.com
Breitling, www.breitling.com
Burberry, www.burberry.com
Bvlgari, www.bvlgari.com
Calvin Klein, www.calvinklein.com
Cartier, www.cartier.com
Casio, www. casio.fr
Celio, www.celio.com
Chanel, www.chanel.com
Chaumet, www.chaumet.com
Chopard, www.chopard.com
Corum, www.corum.ch
D & G Time, www.timeway.ch
Dior, www.dior.com
Dubey & Schaldenbrand,
www.dubeywatch.com

Ebel, www.ebel.com
Eterna, www.eterna.ch
Façonnable, www.faconnable.fr
Fendi, www.fendi.com
Franck Muller,
www.franckmullerusa.com
François-Paul Journe,
www.fpjourne.com
Gérald Charles,
www.geraldcharles.com
Girard-Perregaux,
www.girard-perregaux.ch
Gucci, www.gucci.com
Guess, www.guess.com
Guy Ellia, www.guyellia.com
Harry Winston,
www.harrywinston.com
Hermès, www.hermes.com
Hublot, www.hublot.ch
Hugo Boss,
www.hugoboss.com
IWC, www.iwc.com

Jaeger-leCoultre,
www.jaeger-lecoultre.com
Kenneth Cole,
www.kennethcole.com
Kronotype, www.kronotype.com
L. Leroy, www.l-leroy.com
Lacoste, www.lacoste.com
Lancel, www.lancel.com
Léonard,
www.leonardwatches.com
Longines, www.longines.com
Mercedes,
www.mercedes-benz.lu
Montblanc, www.montblanc.com
Mulberry, www.mulberry.com
Omega,
www.omegawatches.com
Oris, www.oris.ch
Panerai, www.panerai.com
Parmigiani, www.parmigiani.com
Patek Philippe,
www.patekphilippe.com

Piaget, www.piaget.com
Repossi, www.repossi.mc
Richard Mille,
www.richardmille.com
Rolex, www.rolex.com
Salvatore Ferragamo,
www.ferragamo.com
Seiko, www.seiko.fr
ST Dupont, www.st-dupont.com
Swatch, www.swatch.com
TAG Heuer, www.tagheuer.com
Vacheron Constantin,
www.vacheron-constantin.com
Van Cleef & Arpels,
www.vca-jewelers.com
Van Der Bauwede,
www.mvdb.ch
Versace, www.versace.com
Wyler Vetta, www.wylervetta.ch
Yves Saint Laurent, www.ysl.com
Zenith,
www.zenith-watches.com

photographic credits

Corbis *Mark Peterson* 114–115.

Getty images *Altrendo Images* 44 – *Matthew Antrobus* 42–43 –
Jim Arbogast 152 – *Roy Botterell/Taxi* 80 – *Peter Cade* 182–183 –
Rob Goldman/Taxi 78–79 – *Tim Macpherson* 10 – *David Madison* 216–217
– *Antony Nagelmann* 150–151 – *PM Images/Taxi* 8–9 – *Marc Romanelli* 184.

Iconica *Koca* 218.

Zefa/Imageshop *Benno de Wilde* 116.